MW01064073

# VOLLEYBALL

Natasha Evdokimoff

Weigl Publishers Inc.

**Published by Weigl Publishers Inc.**

123 South Broad Street, Box 227

Mankato, MN 56002

USA

Library of Congress Cataloging-in-Publication Data available upon request from the publisher.

Fax: (507) 388-2746 for the attention of the Publishing Records Department

ISBN 1-930954-20-4

Printed in the United States of America

1 2 3  4 5 6 7 8 9  05 04 03 02 01

**Project Coordinator**

Rennay Craats

**Layout and Design**

Warren Clark

**Copy Editor**

Heather Kissock

**Photograph credits**

Cover: Visuals Unlimited (H.Q. Stevens); Title: USA Volleyball (Casey B. Gibson); Contents: Freestyle Photography (Andr Ringuette); Alberta Volleyball: pages 5R, 12L, 16L, 17T, 22; Archive Photos/Hulton-Getty: page 4; Corel Corporation: page 20L; Dave Black: pages 8, 10T; EyeWire: page 21L; Freestyle Photography: pages 5L (Andr Ringuette), 13L (Phillip MacCullum), 16R (Phillip MacCullum), 17B (Phillip MacCullum), 19L (Andr Ringuette), 23 (Andr Ringuette); Globe Photos Inc: page 19R (Henry McGee); Monique de St. Croix: pages 7R, 13R; Newsport Photography Inc: page 18L (William R. Sallaz); Rennay Craats: page 20R; Reuters/ArchivePhotos: 12R (Eriko Sugita), 15L (Win McNamee), 18R (Win McNamee); USA Volleyball: pages 6/7 (Casey B. Gibson), 10B (Don Liebig), 11 (Don Liebig), 15R (Tom Kimmell), 21R (Casey B. Gibson); Visuals Unlimited: pages 14L (Adrian Corton), 14R (H.Q. Stevens).

# Contents

# All About Volleyball

**V**olleyball was invented by William Morgan in 1895. During a trial game, someone said that the ball was volleyed over the net. The game then became known as volleyball. The first game was played at Massachusetts College in 1896. For the first few years, players used a basketball. By 1900, a special ball was designed just for volleyball.

In 1930, the first official outdoor game was played. Outdoor volleyball can be played on grass, but it is most often played on sand. Beach volleyball has developed its own rules and leagues.

Volleyball quickly became popular. By 1900, both men and women were enjoying the sport.

**I** n volleyball, two teams of six stand on opposite sides of a raised net. Players keep a ball in the air by hitting or passing it. Most often the ball is hit with hands, wrists, or arms. To score, a team must get the ball to touch the ground on the other side of the net within the boundary lines.

International league games are played worldwide.

Volleyball has leagues for men and women at all levels. Different rules sometimes apply to different leagues. More than 800 million people play this sport around the world every week!

Beach volleyball is played competitively and for fun.

CHECK IT OUT

To learn more about your favorite sports, check out
**www.members.aol.com/msdaizy/ sports/locker.html**

# What You Will Need

**A** player's uniform must be light so he or she can jump and move fast. It does not take much equipment to play volleyball.

Players usually wear T-shirts. Some players like to wear long sleeves to cushion their arms. Team members all wear the same color. Every player wears a number so the officials can make calls easily.

Players wear pads on their knees and sometimes on their elbows. Pads help to prevent injuries when players dive on the floor for the ball.

A volleyball is made of soft, padded leather. The leather is stitched over rubber and the ball is filled with air. The ball is very light, so hitting it with arms and wrists does not hurt. Volleyballs are usually white, but can be brightly colored for beach games.

A net separates the two teams. A volleyball net is made of **mesh**. The corners are tied to poles to pull the net tight. For adult players, the net is more than 7 feet high. For junior players, it stands just below 7 feet. Two flexible rods called **antennas** stick up at both ends of the net. These rods help show if the ball goes out of bounds while going over the net.

In 1900, a special ball was designed specifically for volleyball. It weighs between 9 and 10 ounces.

Players often wear a pair of gym shorts to play. They are comfortable so players can move quickly and easily.

A pair of good sneakers is important for this game. Sneakers have rubber soles to help prevent slipping when players jump and move for the ball.

# The Court

**V**olleyball is played on a rectangular court. Boundary lines around the court show the court area.

The boundary lines are called side lines and end lines. To score a point, the ball must land inside the boundary. The area outside the boundary is called the **free zone**. If the ball lands in the free zone, it is out of play.

Both indoor and outdoor volleyball courts are the same size.

CHECK IT OUT

To learn more details about the volleyball court, surf to

**www.volleyball.org**

The court is divided into two equal sides by the center line. The net hangs directly above center line. Teams switch sides of the playing court after every game.

Each side of the court has two zones. One is the **front zone** and the other is the **back zone,** or court. The **attack line** separates these zones and shows where players should stand. Players have different jobs to do depending on which zone they stand in.

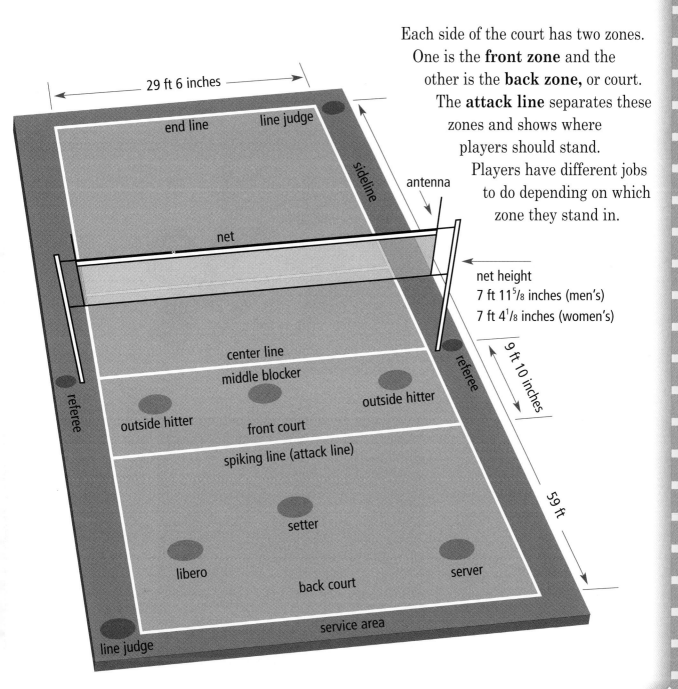

29 ft 6 inches

end line

line judge

sideline

antenna

net

net height
7 ft 11⁵/₈ inches (men's)
7 ft 4¹/₈ inches (women's)

9 ft 10 inches

center line

middle blocker

outside hitter

outside hitter

referee

front court

spiking line (attack line)

59 ft

setter

libero

server

back court

service area

line judge

referee

# Game Basics

**A** volleyball event is called a match. There are often three or five games in a **match**. The team that wins the most games in the match wins.

Volleyball teams often rely on strong hitting, or spiking, to score points and win games.

In most games, the first team to score fifteen points wins. A team must win by two points in regular games. Only the serving team can score points. The server hits the ball over the net. If it touches the ground on the other side within the boundary, the serving team scores one point. If the **serve** touches the net, goes out of bounds, or does not make it over, the team loses possession. If the ball touches the ground on the serving team's side in a **rally**, they lose the serve. No points are scored when this happens. Instead, a **side out** is called and the other team takes a turn at serving.

When players contact the ball with their forearms it is called a bump or a forearm pass. The ball should come off of the arms just above the wrists.

Teams can hit the ball only three times when it is on their side. Players must send the ball back over the net by the third hit. A player cannot hit the ball twice in a row. Players could originally hit the ball only with their upper bodies. A 1996 rule change made it legal to play the ball off the players lower bodies. Not all leagues follow this ruling.

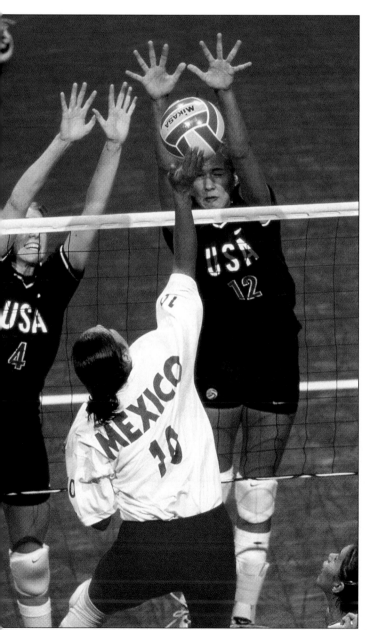

If a player briefly catches or **carries** the ball, it is called a **fault**. Some other faults are reaching over the net, crossing the center line, and touching the net. If the serving team faults, they lose the serve. If the receiving team faults, they get a point scored against them.

Every match has two referees and two line judges. The first referee sits on a raised platform at one end of the net. This gives him or her a clear view of the entire court. The second referee stands on the floor at the other end of the net to watch for low violations. Referees make sure the game rules are followed.

The line judges stand in the free zone on opposite ends and sides of the court. Their job is to decide if the ball lands in or out of bounds. Line judges use flags to show their calls.

Blockers need to watch their opponents' hands, eyes, and shoulders to see where they are going to hit the ball.

# Positions and Plays

**T**eams are made up of six players who stand in two rows. Three stand in the front zone and three stand in the back zone.

Players in the front zone jump at the net to **block** hard hits. They also **spike** the ball onto the other team's side. Back zone players receive serves from the other team. They also **bump** the ball to front zone players, who then try to score.

The server stands at the back of the court, usually to the right. The server steps behind the end line with the ball. He or she then hits the ball overhand or underhand over the net. If he or she steps over the line, the referee calls a foot foul and the team loses its serve. Once the ball is served, the player can step back in bounds.

A spike is a hard shot hit with an open hand. It is directed toward the ground so the opposite team has less time to react and move.

Players have to be very fit. In two-player games, the players must be able to move from the net to the back of the court easily.

**T**eam members pass the ball between each other as they like, up to three times. A **set** is when a player passes the ball lightly off his or her fingertips to another team member. With this move, the ball can be pushed high in the air. A set is also called a volley. A bump is bounced off a player's extended forearms. Bumps are best to pass low balls or return hard serves or spikes.

Beach volleyball allows athletes to play the sport and enjoy the sunshine.

Unlike other athletes, most volleyball players play every position. Liberos, a fairly new position, can pass and dig up hits, but they cannot jump at the net. They are strictly defensive players.

Teams **rotate** positions in a clockwise direction on the court. They rotate whenever the team gets a new turn to serve.

A set is pushed into the air for other players to hit or pass. A good set makes for better spikes.

**CHECK IT OUT**

To read more about performing volleyball skills, check out

**www.freezone.com/sports**

# Where the Action Is

**V**olleyball teams start at the junior high or high school level. There are girls and boys teams in grades seven through twelve. Schools play against each other through the season, competing for the city title.

There are many regional volleyball clubs for young players. Club leagues have teams for girls and boys between seven and eighteen years old. There, players learn the skills they will need for highly competitive play. After high school, many players choose to play on college or university teams. These games are fast paced and fun to watch. Colleges and universities from across the country compete for the national college title.

Volleyball is becoming a popular sport among youth. Many leagues are open to all ages and abilities.

College level players have the opportunity to apply for scholarships and awards

**A**ll serious players would love to represent their country on an Olympic volleyball team. Both indoor and beach volleyball are played at the Summer Olympic Games. Teams from around the world play intense matches in competition for the gold medal.

Beach volleyball became part of the Atlanta Summer Olympics in 1996.

Professional teams get paid to play volleyball. Beach volleyball has professional men's and women's teams. The United States has a professional indoor volleyball league as well.

Success in international competition is a great accomplishment. Team members spend years preparing for this level of play.

CHECK IT OUT

To find out about volleyball camps in your area, check out

**www.kidscamps.com**

# Beach Volleyball

**P**laying volleyball outside has been popular for many years. Outdoor games got started in California and were often played on the beach. Groups of people would make teams and enjoy the game as part of a fun day outside. Soon, beach games became competitive.

Top players from around the world attend events such as the Pan American Games.

At first, the same rules were used for both indoor and outdoor games. Before long, beach volleyball started a separate league with its own rules. In most beach games, there are only two players per team playing on a sand court. Two-person teams guarantee the action will be fast and exciting.

Body position should be low to the ground, with feet pointing straight ahead. This keeps players balanced and ready to react quickly.

**P**layers wear bathing suits and other stretchy clothes to help keep sand off. Because they are in the sun, players often wear sunglasses or visors. Courts are made with soft sand, so no shoes or pads are needed.

Today there are professional beach volleyball leagues all over the world. Players earn prize money for winning games.

Players try to spike the ball. Opposing players jump at the net to stop the ball from getting through them.

Communicating with your partner is one of the most important parts of playing on any sports team.

**CHECK IT OUT**

Read the ins and outs of beach volleyball at
**www.bvbdb.com**

# Stars of the Game

**T**hese are some of the well-known players of this fantastic sport.

## TOM SORENSEN

**LEAGUE:**
National Men's
Indoor Team

### Career Facts:

- Tom played in such competitions as the World League, Pan-American Games, and World Championship matches.
- Tom was named Wisconsin State High School League Most Valuable Player twice.
- Tom ranked number two nationally in 1992 for number of "**kills**" per game.
- Tom held All-American and All-Conference honors during college play.
- Tom was the leading spiker for Team USA's first two World Cup matches.

## KARCH KIRALY

**LEAGUE:**
Professional Men's
Beach Volleyball

### Career Facts:

- In 1984, Karch was the youngest member of the men's Olympic indoor volleyball team.
- Karch was the Olympic indoor team captain in 1988. The team won the gold medal.
- In 1991, Karch was named the World Championship Most Valuable Player.
- Karch became a professional beach player in 1991.
- Karch has won all five major professional beach tournaments.
- In 1996, Karch won Olympic gold in the beach volleyball competition.

## PAUL DUERDEN

**LEAGUE:**
Canadian National
Team

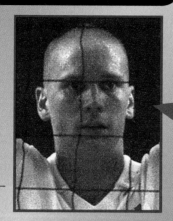

### Career Fact:

- Paul has played in more than 200 international games.
- In 1992, Paul made Canada's National team at eighteen years old.
- Because he is a young player, Paul's teammates call him "The Kid."
- Paul is considered one of the top five attackers, or spikers, in the world.
- Paul played professional volleyball in France. His team won the French league and the European Cup in 2000.

## GABRIELLE REECE

**LEAGUE:**
Professional Women's
Beach Volleyball

### Career Facts:

- Gabrielle was the leader in game "kills" for the 1994, 1995, and 1996 seasons.
- In 1994 and 1995, Gabrielle was the Offensive Player of the Year.
- Gabrielle is ranked fifth in the National College Athletic Association (NCAA) for career blocks.
- Gabrielle has been her team's captain for five seasons.
- Gabrielle also works as a fashion model and television announcer.

# Be at Your Best

**A**healthy diet helps people be strong athletes. Fruits and vegetables provide many of the vitamins people need. Breads, pasta, and rice are sources of food energy. Meats have protein for building muscles. Dairy products have calcium, which keeps bones strong. Eating foods from all the food groups everyday will keep a player's body in top condition.

Drinking plenty of water before, during, and after playing sports is important. Water keeps people's bodies cool and running well. When athletes sweat, they lose water. Water replaces what is lost through sweat during a game.

Strong and flexible muscles are important for playing well. Training the right muscles a few times every week makes playing more fun and helps prevent injuries. Stretching keeps muscles flexible. It is best to stretch after a **warm up**. Running in place for a few minutes or doing some laps gets muscles warm.

Strong legs are needed for quick movements. For strong legs, players practice jumping in place. They pull their knees up as high as they can on each jump.

Lunges are other great exercises for stretching leg muscles. Standing with their feet slightly apart, players shift their weight to one side and bend their knee. The other leg stays straight and stretches out.

Players need strong hands and fingers, too. To work these muscles, they squeeze a tennis ball in each hand several times. Players also stretch their shoulder muscles to prepare for hitting and passing the ball.

Stretching with a team member or trainer can help prevent pulled muscles.

CHECK IT OUT

To find out more about the benefits of stretching and healthy eating, check **www.tdclub.com/ysnim/home/**

21

# Volleyball Brain Teasers

**B**rush up on your facts! Read these questions and answers to learn more about this popular sport.

**Q** How old is the sport of volleyball?

**A** Volleyball was first created in 1895, making it more than one hundred years old.

**Q** From what sports does volleyball draw its skills?

**A** Volleyball draws on the same kinds of skills used in handball, basketball, and tennis. Players use their hands, pass the ball between each other, and need to get the ball over a net.

**Q** What kind of net was first used for volleyball matches?

**A** The first games were played using a tennis net. The net was raised off the ground to give it the right height. Before long, special nets were made just for volleyball.

**Q** What was the occupation of volleyball's inventor?

**A** William Morgan was the fitness instructor at the YMCA in Holyoke, Massachusetts. He created the game for Y-members who were looking for a new non-contact sport.

**Q** When did volleyball become an Olympic sport?

**A** Indoor volleyball was introduced to the Olympic Games in Tokyo in 1964. Beach volleyball became an Olympic sport in 1996.

**Q** What are some variations to volleyball?

**A** Not only are there indoor and outdoor versions of the game, there is also a 9-player version and a game called Wallyball. This is played in a racquetball court and players can hit the ball off the walls. These games use basic volleyball skills but some of the rules are slightly different.

# Glossary

**antennas:** flexible rods on the net that help show when the ball goes out of bounds

**attack line:** the line that divides the front and back zones

**back zone:** the area between the attack and end lines

**block:** when players jump up at the net to stop a hard spike from the other team

**bump:** a pass where the ball contacts the forearms; arms are straight and hands are joined

**carries:** holds the ball instead of letting it bounce quickly off the fingertips

**fault:** an illegal move or play called by an official

**free zone:** the area outside the end lines and side lines

**front zone:** the court area between the attack line and center line

**kills:** strong hits that result in points; usually done by spiking the ball

**match:** a series of three or five games

**mesh:** fine rope linked together forming a loose kind of screen

**rally:** a series of hits over the net between teams

**rotate:** clock-wise movement teams make before serving the ball; occurs after a side out is called

**serve:** an overhand or underhand hit that gets the ball over the net from behind the end line

**set:** a soft hit with the fingertips that can send the ball high into the air; also called a volley

**side out:** the call made when the serving team commits a fault, causing them to lose the right to serve

**spike:** a hard, downward hit made above the net, aimed at the opponent's side of the court

**warm up:** gentle exercise to get your body ready for stretching and game play

# Index